Book Power
Year 1

Literacy through Literature

Jane Bunting

With contributions from Sue McGonigle and Ann Ross

CD materials by Olivia O'Sullivan

clpe
Centre for Literacy
in Primary Education

ISBN 9781 872267 456

© Copyright 2008

Centre for Literacy in Primary Education
Webber Street
London SE1 8QW
Telephone: 020 7401 3382/3
info@clpe.co.uk
www.clpe.co.uk

Contents

Introducing the key teaching approaches:
Using texts as the core of a literacy programme

The children's books featured in this book all lend themselves to being talked and thought about in depth in the Year One classroom. They have been chosen because they are powerful stories which are likely to engage children, stir their ideas and feelings and involve them in discussion.

Each book is the focus of a unit of work that lasts for between three to six weeks providing opportunities for a wide range of work in literacy. Working in this way means that children can get to know a book really well.

The approaches suggested here are designed to enable children to respond to the books more intensively and to reflect on them in a variety of ways including through talk and writing. In addition young writers learn a lot about writing from their reading and can use these texts as a starting point and inspiration for their own writing.

Reading aloud

Reading aloud is probably the most important thing that teachers can do and needs to be a frequent and regular part of each school day.

Reading aloud slows written language down and enables children to hear and take in the tunes and patterns of it. It enables children to experience and enjoy stories they might otherwise not meet. By reading well-chosen books aloud, teachers help classes to become communities of readers. As such they can share in experiences of a wide repertoire of books they enjoy and get to know well. Subsequent conversations about books help children to explore and reflect on stories in ways that are made meaningful, personal and pleasurable.

Before reading a book to a class, teachers should read it for themselves: in this way they can think about the best way to read it. If children are to respond to the tunes and the meanings of a book

it needs to be read aloud in a way that engages the listener.

Re-reading

Opportunities for re-reading a book that they have listened to helps all children to engage more deeply with it. Reading and re-reading known texts is very important for all readers, but particularly for less experienced readers or those for whom English is an additional language as it helps them to be able to read at least parts of it confidently for themselves.

Three important times for children to revisit books are during shared reading, group reading and independent reading. Teachers are encouraged to provide for all of these in these units because they provide supported opportunities to extend conversations about the books.

Responding and reflecting

The following approaches help children to respond to the questions:

How do you like this book?
What does it make you think/feel?
What do you think it all means?

They encourage children to reflect on the meanings of the text that they are reading, to recognise and explore their own responses to it and to begin to develop their understanding of what the writer has to say.

Booktalk

Discussion about books forms the foundations for working around texts.

Children need frequent, regular and sustained opportunities to talk together about the books that they are reading as a whole class. The more experience they have of talking together like this the better they get at making explicit the meanings that a text holds for them: a child quoted in *'Tell Me': Children, Reading & Talk* by Aidan Chambers in which Booktalk is best portrayed says, 'we don't know what we think about a book until we've talked about it'.

This Booktalk is supportive to all readers and writers, but it is especially empowering for children who find literacy difficult. It helps the class as a whole to reach shared understandings and move towards a more dispassionate debate of ideas and issues.

In this book we offer suggestions for the sorts of questions that teachers and children might use in discussion. These questions are shown in italics.

Getting the talk started by asking the basic questions

Once they have heard a book read aloud, the class can begin to explore their response to it

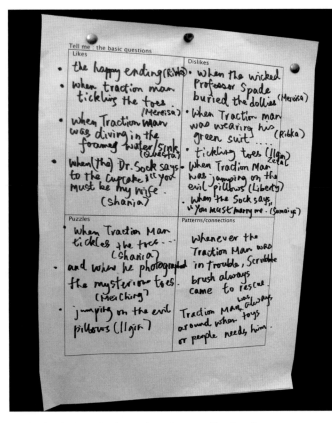

with the help of what Chambers calls the four basic questions. These questions give children accessible starting points for discussion:

'Tell me… was there anything you liked about this book….?'
'Was there anything that you particularly disliked..?'
'Was there anything that puzzled you?'
'Were there any patterns….any connections that you noticed…?'

The openness of these questions unlike the more interrogative 'why' question encourages every child to feel that they have something to say, and allows everyone to take part in arriving at a shared view.

As children reply it can be useful to write down what they say under the headings 'likes', 'dislikes', 'puzzles', 'patterns'. This written record helps to map out the class's view of the important meanings and is a way of holding on to ideas for later.

This is an especially useful way to begin working on a new story or book and will lead children inevitably into a fuller discussion using more general and focussed questions. Once children are used to working with the 'Tell me' questions they can use them for themselves when talking about their reading with each other.

Asking the 'special' questions

'Tell me' also contains suggestions for 'special questions' to use once discussion has taken off. These are questions which direct children's attention more closely to themes or ideas that are particularly important to an understanding of the story, but which might otherwise be overlooked.

The class reading journals

Class reading journals provide a collective thinking space for children to explore and reflect on their reading experience through shared writing and drawing. Talking about what they have read together helps them to clarify their thoughts and helps them begin to articulate some of what they think and feel.

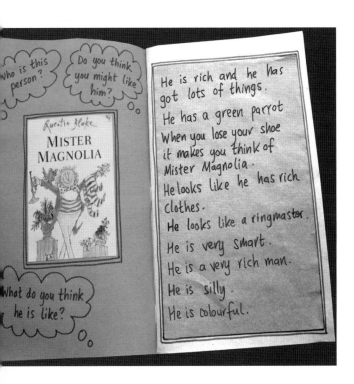

Interpreting and performing

The following key teaching approaches help children to interpret the meanings that the text holds for them, using a variety of expressive means including dance, music and art.

They help children to answer the questions:

What kind of meanings does this story/poem have for you?
How can we bring out these meanings for others?

Storytelling and retelling

Retelling a story is a powerful way for children to make a story their own. Storytelling helps children concentrate on the best way to tell the story, and to make deliberate choices about the words and phrases they use in the telling. All of this will help greatly when they come to writing.

When a story is familiar it is easier for a reader to get hold of its shape, and to consider how it fits together. Children can use storyboards or story maps as supports for their retelling. These techniques help them identify the 'bones' of the story. Longer stories can be 'passed around' a story circle : children build confidence by telling a small chunk of the story and then passing it on to the next person.

Drama and role-play

Drama and role-play provide immediate routes into the world of a story and allow children to explore texts actively. They enable children to put themselves into a particular character's shoes and imagine how things would look from that point of view. Through drama and role-play children can imagine characters' body language, behaviour and tones of voice, in ways that they can draw on later when they write.

Freeze-frame

Freeze-frames are still images or tableaux. They can be used to enable groups of children to examine a key event or situation from a story and decide in detail how it could be represented. When presenting the freeze-frame, one of the group could act as a commentator to talk through what is happening in their version of the scene, or individual characters could be asked to speak their thoughts out loud.

Hot seating

In hot seating, one of the class role-plays a key character from a poem or story and is interviewed by the rest. This activity involves children in examining a character's motivation closely. Before the hot seating, children need to discuss what they want to know in order to identify questions and ideas that they want answering. If children have no experience of hot seating the teacher may initially need to take the role.

Writing in role

When children have explored a fictional situation through talk or role-play they may be ready to write in role as a character in a story. Taking the role of a particular character enables even very young writers to see events from that viewpoint and involves them in writing in a different voice. In role, children can often access feelings and language that are not available to them when they write as themselves.

Performing poetry

All poetry needs to be lifted off the page and given voice. Whether they are reading or writing poetry it helps if children work with performance in mind. Children invited to prepare poems for performance may choose to enliven them by using a rhythmic or musical accompaniment to the words.

Visualising

Asking children to picture or to 'visualise' a character or place from a story is a way of encouraging them to move into a fictional world. Children can be asked to picture the scene in their mind's eye or 'walk around it' in their imagination. Once they have done so, they can bring it to life by describing it in words or recreating it in drawing or painting.

This is a way for children to begin to articulate their response to what they read and can help children to analyse the ways in which the writer has used language and images to create a world.

Drawing and annotating

Opportunities to draw before and during writing increase young children's motivation, and can help them to think. Drawing can help all writers plan their writing and develop their ideas.

Drawing and annotating settings

Drawing story settings prompts children to imagine what a scene looks like, or visualise it from a particular viewpoint.

Drawing and annotating characters

Drawing characters focuses attention on them how they look, what they say, how they behave. To support their idea of what a character is like children have to refer to the text. They can also be encouraged to draw on the language of the text in making annotations around the drawings.

Responding to illustration

All of the books in this book have been chosen because of the quality of the illustrations they contain and the ways in which they work with the text to create meaning for the reader. Children will need time and opportunity to enjoy and respond to the pictures, and to talk together about what they contribute to their understanding of the texts. There could be opportunities for children to develop their responses by drawing or painting in a similar style to the illustrations.

Illustrating the text

Opportunities to illustrate a story during an activity such as bookmaking give children the chance to draw on the ideas that they have gained from talk, storymaking, role-play and drawing. They enable children to engage in creative reinterpretations of the text.

Shared writing

Shared writing is possibly the most important way a teacher can help all children to experience what it is like to be a writer.

Acting as scribe, the teacher works with a group of children to create a text. Teacher and children work together as active partners, talking together to share ideas. The teacher guides the children through all the decisions that writers need to make and helps them shape their thoughts on paper.

This gives children a model for their own independent writing and results in clear literary outcomes such as a poster, Big Book or poem that everyone can enjoy.

Book making

Publishing their work for an audience helps children to write more purposefully. Book making provides a motivating context within which children can bring together their developing understandings of what written language is like; making written language meaningful as they construct their own texts. The decisions that all writers have to take and the processes of redrafting, editing and punctuation can be demonstrated and discussed as teachers and children write together in shared writing.

Small world play

Opportunities for small world play that are based on a known story promote talk about the shape of the story, encourage children to discuss key elements such as character and plot and to make decisions about how they create the setting. As they play whether as individuals or in cooperation with others they practise their narrative skills and 'try on' the different characters using different voices to bring them to life.

Story boxes

Story boxes create particular opportunities to revisit and develop the themes and storylines of a particular story. Typically, they consist of a shoebox containing a range of small toys and inspirational objects. The box itself can be turned into a setting for the story using a variety of collage materials and with sides cut to fold down. However, the box is at its most effective when something intriguing or unexpected is added. Children can use the box to (story)tell the next episode of a story or create another story with a similar setting or characters.

Re-enactment through play

Revisiting stories through a range of play-based experiences helps children to step into the world that someone else has created and to explore it more completely.

Role-play areas

Linking the role-play area to a known story provides important opportunities for children to really get inside the story. As they play the story it helps them to understand its structure, allows them to put themselves into a character's shoes and to think, talk and behave like that character. It encourages them to experiment with the 'what if' of the plot and make it their own. If the role-play area is set up with the children's help they will be involved in thinking about the detail of this fictional world, in making decisions about what this world should be like, and illuminate it with their own experience.

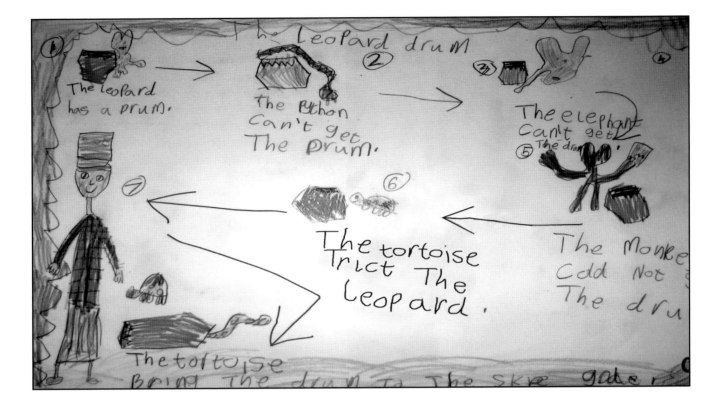

Exploring and analysing text

This section features the key teaching approaches that aim to help children to think about the questions:

How does this text work?
How is it made?

When exploring a story in terms of its language and structure, and how these contribute to its meanings, it is important to build on children's spontaneous interest in language and plan investigative work around it following the interests of the children.

The approaches that follow help children pay close attention to aspects of the way the text is shaped, and consider individual and specific features of plot, structure or language.

Mapping

Mapping a story and its setting helps to develop a sense of the story world.

Maps of story settings

Mapping story settings is a way of establishing the geography of a story more securely and visualising where its characters and events would be located. These kinds of maps can be drawn by pairs, groups, individuals, or by the teacher, drawing on a flip chart or interactive whiteboard to construct a map or plan.

Story maps

Making a story map is a way of retelling the story. It is a graphic means of breaking a story down into episodes and sequencing its events. This kind of graphic representation helps children to hold on to the shape of the story more confidently so that

Talking together as a whole class about how you might collect 'evidence' in this kind of way helps children to see patterns in texts. A chart could help with comparing story beginnings or looking at different characters.

Debate and argument

Talking together about books following the 'Tell me' questions is a very powerful way to explore and reflect on emotional response to a story and what it means for us as individuals. In contrast, debating ideas calls for a more formal and objective response to the story and helps children begin to analyse how the writer has made us feel this way.

Teachers can structure debates inviting 'for' and 'against' arguments around particular statements arising from a book.

Looking at language

Text-marking

In text-marking the group is asked to highlight particular lines or words that they like from the story they are reading and to say what it is they like about them in particular. If this is not something that they are used to doing the teacher may need to start them off with a reflective comment of their own to encourage children to focus on the language in a similar way.

Word Collections

The making of word collections is a way of focusing on the language of a story or poem. Children could make collections of words that describe a particular character's feelings, or, they can collect words that describe a place or situation.

Collecting words in this way helps children to have a more focused awareness of the ways language affects our perceptions and understandings of character and the ways in which the author creates the readers' response.

they can retell it orally or in writing. Children can also make story maps as a form of planning, to prepare for their own writing.

Storyboards

A storyboard is another way of helping to map out key scenes in the story through drawing and annotation. Originally used to plot scenes in film it is particularly useful for marking out the key scenes in a story within a given number of frames, or for focussing in on the next few moments in a sequence.

Drawing up comparison charts

A comparison chart is a visual way of recording similarities or differences in style, language or content, for example when considering the question:

How is this version of the story like that one?

Beegu
Alexis Deacon

A teaching sequence of 4 to 5 weeks

Learning aims

- To engage children with a moving story with which they will empathise

- To discuss the themes and issues that arise, enabling children to make connections with their own lives

- To develop creative responses to the text through play, drama and drawing

- To write in role in order to explore character

Links with PNS objectives

- To retell stories, ordering events using story language
- To explore familiar themes and characters through improvisation and role-play
- To make predictions showing an understanding of ideas, events and characters
- To write for purpose, pleasure and learning

Key Teaching Approaches

Responding to illustration

Booktalk

Re-enactment through play

Storytelling

Debate and argument

Drama and role-play

Shared writing

Writing in role

Book making

This is a deceptively simple picture book which deals with the very large themes of separation, loss, hope and difference.

Beegu is a small alien creature who is stranded on earth when her spaceship crashes. She wants to be friendly and needs to find somewhere where she can belong. Unfortunately the Earth People don't seem to be at all friendly. The story takes its readers through her search for friendship and acceptance, and her experience of repeated rejection. Even when she finds acceptance and solace among other small ones like herself, the adults force her out again. She continues her search until eventually she is found and reunited with her parents.

The illustrations in this book communicate subtly how hostile and strange the world can feel to small people. In many ways Beegu stands for 'every child'. There is much in her story that will chime with any child's own experience as well as offering an opportunity for the whole class to consider together what it would feel like to come to a strange and unfamiliar land where everything is different and unknown.

Responding to illustration

Show the class the picture on the title page and ask them to talk together in pairs about their initial responses to it, either working as a class around the interactive whiteboard, or in groups with laminated copies of the picture.

How does this picture make you feel?
What do you want to know?
What do you think has happened?
What sort of story are you expecting?

Bring the class back together again to share these first impressions and questions, listing them on a flip chart and discussing some of the children's responses and questions more fully.

Read the story aloud to the end.

Spend some time as a class looking carefully at the detail of the pictures, talking together about what is happening and the feelings that are evoked. The pictures in this book communicate the complexities of Beegu's story very clearly.

Look again at the list you made of the children's first responses.

To what extent did the story answer their anxieties and questions?

Booktalk, the class reading journal

Read the story aloud again.
Discuss with the children their responses to the story. Use the 'Tell me' questions to encourage children to express their opinions.

Was there anything that you particularly liked or disliked?

Was there anything that puzzled you?

Give children post-it notes to write down their responses to one or two of these questions. Collect all their responses together into the class reading journal. Some of these responses can be scribed into the journal as a shared writing activity. In this way, the class reading journal can be used to capture the main ideas from each class discussion as you read and talk about the book together. Leave room for children to add their own contributions, either as drawings or as written comment.

This will enable the class to reflect on their own learning at the end of the work.

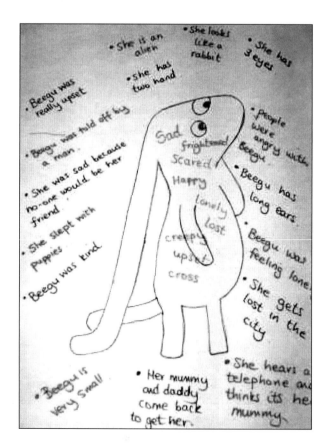

Drawing and annotating

Ask children to draw an outline of Beegu and, working in pairs, to write:
- outside the outline everything that they think they know about her;
- inside the outline words or phrases that show how she is feeling during the time she is on Earth in the story.

Bring the children back together and collect some of the children's words and phrases into an enlarged outline. This will provide a useful opportunity to discuss both the meanings of the words and how they are spelt.

Display this word hoard in the writing area for the children to draw on when writing independently.

Visualising and painting

What do you think Beegu's home planet is like?

Ask the children to shut their eyes and imagine what Beegu's own world might be like. Ask them to turn to a partner and tell them what they see. Children should now paint a picture of this world working as individuals or in pairs. When these are finished invite some children to talk about their ideas to the rest of the class, using their painting as a prompt.

Re-enactment through play

Talk with the children about how they might transform the role-play area into a spaceship, making a list together to help them plan the work

about what it will look like and what props they will need to make. When it is finished discuss with the children what sorts of writing material they think they would find in a spaceship and set time aside for children to make examples of these such as star maps, a captain's logbook, a Martian newspaper or letters from home. Look again together at the ways in which Beegu's talk is depicted within the book: some children may enjoy creating an alien language to write in, perhaps using another font.

Re-enactment through story boxes

Make a story box creating a space setting by using a shoebox and filling it with small story prop models of spaceships and non-terrestrial inhabitants. Children can use textured materials such as mod-roc or papier-mâché to make the surface of the planet and incorporate photographs or other images into the design.

Session eight:

Storytelling

Sit the class in a large ring to retell the story, passing the story around from child to child. Each teller has a minute before handing the story on to the next child to take over the storytelling. Pause occasionally to invite groups of children into the middle of the circle to act out significant scenes from the story.

Session nine:

Drama and role-play

Put the children into groups of five or six to replay the playground scene with children acting in role as the teacher, the child who told, Beegu and the other schoolchildren. At a given signal each group should freeze-frame the moment when the teacher seizes Beegu. Divide the class into two to present their work to the other half of the class. This time each group in turn should hold the freeze-frame while each character within it is lightly touched and asked to say what they are thinking or feeling.

Afterwards discuss with the class how they think Beegu feels.

Session ten:

Debate and argument

Discuss with the children as a class why they think the little girl went to fetch the teacher, and what they think the teacher should have done.

Put the children into pairs to discuss whether they think the teacher was right and why, using a comparison chart to record their discussion.

Session eleven:

Role-play

Put the children into threes and ask them to act out the end of the story when Beegu is reunited with her mum and dad. Invite some of the class to present their role-play to the rest of the class. What do the children think of this ending?

Children should go on to write the conversation that the family had together as speech bubbles for inclusion in the class journal or to be pinned up as part of the display.

Session twelve:

Writing in role

Ask children to write and draw the sort of post-card that Beegu might write back to 'the small ones' after she returns home.

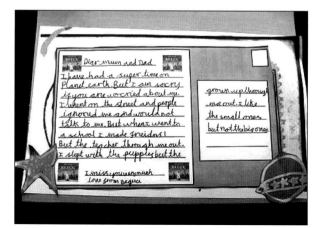

Sessions thirteen and fourteen:

Shared writing

Using shared writing on a flip chart and with you acting as scribe to help shape the class's ideas, write the story from the viewpoint of Beegu, as if she was telling it. This will provide lots of opportunities to talk with the class about some of the decisions that writers have to make. These will include demonstrating how writers sometimes change both ideas and words during the writing. It will also provide a meaningful context for looking at spelling and punctuation. Once the story is finished ask the children to illustrate it and make it into a book for everyone to enjoy.

Session fifteen:

Book making

Prepare small home-made books for children to use to write their own stories. Talk together as a class about possible ideas that they have: some children will want to retell the Beegu story, some may want to write another Beegu adventure while others will want to write and illustrate a space story of their own. When they are finished place them in the book corner where they can become resources for children's own independent reading.

Session sixteen:

Comparing stories

Do you know any other stories like this?

Talk with the children about other space stories that they know. In addition to other stories they have read they will suggest a variety of 'alien' stories that they know from TV and film. Watching some of these together will provide a shared focus for talking further about this genre. Watch the beginning of ET directed by Stephen Spielberg. In it ET is left behind and discovered by the children.

Discuss with the class the ways in which the film creates atmosphere and suspense and develops our sympathies for the alien character, before going on to watch and enjoy the whole film together as a serial film during storytime.

Session seventeen:

Final assembly: Performing the drama

Present Beegu's story to the rest of the school, as if told by Beegu herself and complete with the children's own reflections on her plight. This book provides an important context for exploring with all age-groups the experience of the more vulnerable children within our schools such as those of refugee and asylum-seeking families.

Beegu was not supposed to
be here.

She was lost.

Traction Man is Here
Mini Grey

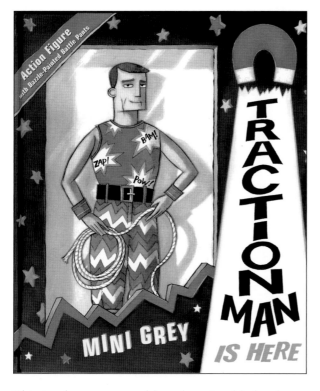

This is a humorous and hugely enjoyable book which captures the way that children interact with action figures and create imaginative play around them.

It tells the story of intrepid hero Traction Man and his faithful side-kick Scrubbing Brush. The two are always ready to launch into battle with the enemies that lurk all around us - in the kitchen sink, the bathtub or the kitchen cupboard. That is, until the day that granny presents Traction Man with a home-made knitted green romper suit. How the two heroes deal with and overcome this innocent attempt to lay them low is the subject of the adventure that follows which, like all good adventure stories, leaves the door ajar for a sequel.

The comic-style pictures of the book teem with action and detail. Children will pore over them for hours, excitedly discussing them together.

A teaching sequence of 3 weeks

Learning aims

- To develop creative responses to a book through play, drama and drawing

- To explore ideas, and to listen to and respond to others' contributions

- To read for pleasure and enjoyment

- To combine drawing and writing to create a multi-modal text

Links with PNS objectives

- To retell stories, ordering events and using story language

- To explore themes and characters through improvisation and role-play

- To choose independently what to write about, plan and follow it through

- To create texts on paper and screen

Key Teaching Approaches

Responding to illustration

Booktalk

Re-enactment through play

Drama and role-play

Bookmaking

Debate and argument

Drawing and annotating

Shared writing

Responding to illustration

Read this book straight through until the page where the family are unwrapping their presents at granny's house so that children can clearly hear the distinctive way that the story is written. Talk with the children about what they think each of the family is thinking as they unwrap their presents.

On a flip chart or using prepared speech bubbles write down some of these suggestions as speech bubbles. Finally, put the children into pairs to go into role as Traction Man and Scrubbing Brush as they unwrap granny's present and put on the green romper suit.
Ask them to 'freeze' the final frame of this sequence.
Go round the class asking pairs to say what they are thinking at this point.

Read to the end of the story.

Booktalk

Talk with the children about their first responses to the book. Return to particular pages, talking together about the pictures and re-reading the parts of the story that children have particularly enjoyed.
Using shared writing, write down some of what they say into a class reading journal that you have already prepared.

Re-enactment through play

Collect together the props for each of Traction Man's adventures - the defeat of the evil pillows, the kitchen sink drama, the relief of the garden dollies, bath time and the rescue of the spoons - and place them in the sand, water, or outside area for children to use in their own storymaking.

Drama and role-play

Cast different groups of children into each of Traction Man's adventures. Sitting in a large circle read the story again. Invite each group of children to come into the centre of the circle to act out their part of the book.

Re-enactment through play and bookmaking

Take one of the play settings from the story and recreate it within a story box by filling it with a collection of appropriate models and props. Include a wider collection than those included within the book so that children can use them to develop their ideas and create their own stories. When they are finished children should use the boxes to tell their stories to either their own or other classes. They could also make a photographic version of the story, photographing each story box scene and making it into a book, perhaps with written captions.

ICT and bookmaking

Make electronic versions of the finished story box stories using PowerPoint, and adding photographs, children's pictures and a combination of recorded voice and text. These can be stored in a folder on the school network and made into CDs for children to take home.

Debate and argument

Talk with children about what they think a hero is and whether they think Traction Man is one.

What other stories about heroes do they know?

Put children in pairs to tell each other about their own favourite hero, and to discuss what they think he or she does that makes him/her heroic. Bring the group back together and list these ideas into the class reading journal.

Drawing and annotating, shared writing

Have an action toy open day when children bring their favourite toy into school for the day and introduce it to the class. Give each child a timed slot to talk about their toy and why they think it is a hero. Take photos of them both together. Ask children to make an annotated drawing of their toy. Using shared writing devise an ID permit together for each child to write on behalf of their toy. Children who do not have a figure of their own can create the one they would ideally like. Bind these into books and place them in the book corner.

Illustrating and annotating

Suggest children choose a hero to paint and when they have finished select six words or phrases that describe what he or she is like. Display these around each painting.

Re-reading

Make a collection of stories about superheroes for children to read and talk about together. These could include heroes of television and film as well as those from comics and other graphic books.

Writing comic strips

Re-read the story again, this time focusing on the ways in which pictures and text combine to tell the story.

How is this book similar and dissimilar to a comic?

Using shared writing make a large size comic with the class. Invite children to draw particular frames of the story or stick in drawings of particular characters. Ask children to write the graphics using large felt-tipped pens.

Children can now work in pairs to write and draw a comic adventure for Traction Man, either using one of the stories from the book as the basis, or creating a new one. When the comics are finished, laminate them and place them in the book corner.

Responding to illustration

Put the picture showing Traction Man in his unwrapped box up onto the interactive white-board. Ask children to imagine that they have just unwrapped this present. What words would they use to describe how they are feeling?

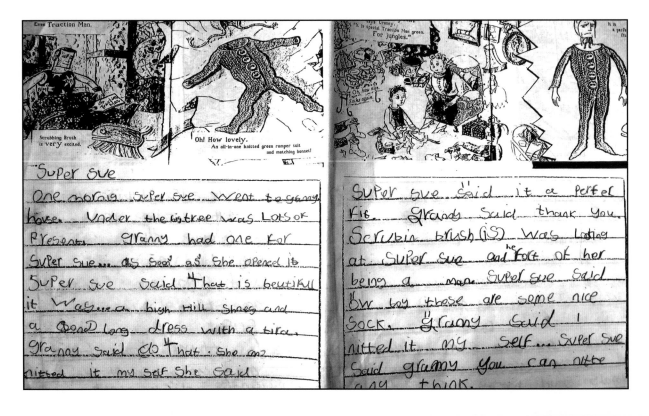

Session thirteen:

Drama and role-play

Put children into groups of four to improvise what happens next. Use the last picture in the book as the starting point for their drama of the next adventure. Each group should present their work in turn to the rest of the class for them to comment on what they liked about each other's ideas. They can go on to re-work and develop them further.

Sessions fourteen and fifteen:

Shared writing and performance

Using shared writing and drawing on ideas from the children's own dramas, write a play version as a class for the next adventure. You will need to decide together how much of the story can be told through the characters and what they do, and how much by the narrator (or narrators). Use instruments to improvise the 'film score' to accompany the performance and present it as a finished performance in assembly.

Talk with them about how the design of the box contributes to their responses. Focusing on the colours, graphics and use of language ask them what they think is particularly effective.

Look together at some other toy packaging or toy advertisements. Talk together about the ways in which the design works to capture their attention. What is it about the ways in which the toy is presented that they especially like?

If they wanted someone to buy their favourite hero what would they draw and write on the box?

Children can go on to design and make their own packaging for their own favourite toy.

The Owl and the Pussy Cat
Edward Lear and Louise Voce

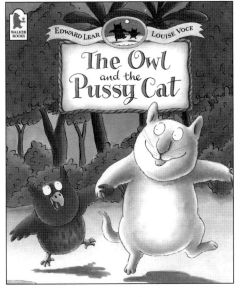

A teaching sequence of 3 to 4 weeks

Learning aims

- To respond creatively to a long narrative poem

- To explore and develop ideas through talk

- To read independently for purpose, pleasure and learning

- To use work in role to explore ideas and texts

The Owl and the Pussy Cat, one of the most famous and best-loved of Edward Lear's classic nonsense verses, is known for its light-hearted absurdity and some nonsensical language. However, light-hearted as it undoubtedly is, it also has something important to say about friendship and the way we are with others.

The poem tells the story of the epic sea voyage of two strangely mismatched but star-struck lovers and their eventual marriage on the island of the Bong Tree. On the way we meet some of child-hood's unforgettable characters: the piggy-wig and his ring and the turkey who lives on the hill and who marries them. We also get to dance at a wedding party where we eat with a runcible spoon.

There have been many illustrated versions of the poem and children will enjoy exploring and discussing the different ways in which the gallant pair's adventures have been portrayed. Here Louise Voce's clear, vibrant and engaging illustrations which perfectly capture the spirit of this nonsensical masterpiece sparkle. They also give children the perfect portal through which to explore it.

Links with PNS objectives

- To read and write for a range of purposes on paper and on screen
- To respond imaginatively using different strategies to engage with texts
- To act out a well-known story, using voices for characters
- To visualise and comment on events, characters and ideas

Key Teaching Approaches

Bookmaking

Visualising

Story mapping

Storytelling

Performing poetry

Re-enactment through play

Shared writing

Introducing the book: reading aloud and re-reading

Read the poem straight through pausing occasionally as you do so to talk with the children about some of the pictures and to use them to help make sense of the less familiar language. It will be helpful to have collected together some props and artefacts to support the poem beforehand so that the children can see what these are like.

You might, for example, have models of all the characters, show a quince or a photograph of one, or even have ready some quince jelly to taste on bread.

Re-read the poem inviting the children to join in.

Another way to introduce the poem is to present the children with the collection of objects before reading the poem. Invite them to be 'story detectives' exploring and speculating about what the objects are and what sort of story could be told with props like these.

After the discussion read the poem aloud.

Bookmaking

Give out different sections of the poem to pairs of children to read and illustrate using collage, paint or drawing. When the pictures are finished bind them alongside the text of the poem to make the class's own Big Book version or make a wall story pinning the pictures and text up along the wall. Encourage children to read along with it during the day.

These pictures could then be easily transferred into Powerpoint, and, with the addition of a sound file of the children reading the poem, made into a talking book to use through the interactive whiteboard. You might also make a tape of the class reading it aloud to keep with the book itself in the book/listening corner. Place it somewhere where children can easily choose to read or listen to it.

Reading in role

Divide the class into Owls, Pussy Cats, Piggy-wigs and narrators and read the poem aloud together using an enlarged version of the text. Being grouped with more confident readers will support children who are less confident readers and also encourage them to read more expressively.
Make magnetic or puppet story props with the less confident readers for everybody to use when retelling the story.

Performing the Owl and Pussy Cat song

Teach the class to sing the poem using any of the existing published tunes or improvise your own using a tune the class already know.

Story mapping and retelling

In pairs and working on large sheets of paper ask children to draw a map of the story, starting with all the features that they know about from the song. Encourage them to work in detail. Children should go on to annotate their maps, first adding speech bubbles for their characters and then writing a story beginning and a story end to fit their own version. They should stick these onto the start and finish of their maps. When finished, invite pairs of children to storytell their stories to the rest of the class using their maps as a guide. Children can use the maps as a plan for writing a narrative version of the story later.

Visualising, painting and writing postcards home

Sit in a circle and sing the song straight through with everybody miming all the actions as you sing. Pass a telescope around and ask children what they imagine they can see through it. Ask children to talk with the person next to them about the things they can see before inviting someone to describe their picture in enough detail for you to draw it as they talk. Children can now work in pairs or as individuals to paint their own 'through the telescope' picture. When they are finished suggest children write a postcard home to tell friends or family about their travels.

Reading and re-reading

Make a collection of other Edward Lear nonsense poems such as 'The Quangle Wangle's Hat', 'The Dong with the Luminous Nose' or 'The Jumblies' as well as other illustrated editions of 'The Owl and the Pussy Cat'. Children can select from these to share together in their independent reading. Include props such as masks or puppets for them to use alongside the books. Choose a poem from this selection to read aloud every day; children will then quickly come to know many of them off by heart and establish firm personal favourites. Make some of these into songsheets to read with the class, in guided reading, or to keep in the bookcorner for children's independent reading.

Re-enactment through play

Suggest to the class that they turn the role-play area into either the boat that the Owl and the Pussy Cat used on their epic trip, or the land where the Bong Tree grows. Discuss with them what they would need to do and what props they would need to make, capturing their ideas as a list. Children can then check these off as they complete each task. They should also add on any other ideas they have as they develop the area.

Both scenarios present ample reasons for children to write as part of their play especially when particular materials and examples of writing are introduced into the area. Sometimes you will need to write alongside them yourself in the role-play area in order to give them particular ideas, for example, writing a treasure map or a message in a bottle. Other sorts of writing benefit from being given more formal support, for example, creating a mermaid poem or song in guided or shared writing.

Sessions eleven and twelve:

Shared writing

Using shared writing, write the diary of the Owl and the Pussy Cat's long journey to the land

where the Bong Tree grows. Have a large empty book already prepared to use as the ship's log, and each day write into it one day's entry, with you acting as scribe to discuss and help shape the children's ideas. Before writing each day's entry you might hot seat one child to be the Owl or the Pussy Cat and ask them to come along to tell everyone what they saw or did on that day.

Session thirteen:

Performing poetry

Act out the poem improvising and adding to some of the scenes such as the sea-journey or the Owl and the Pussy Cat's activities on the island. First as individuals and then in pairs ask children to make up the wedding dance. Children can compose their own musical accompaniment for this using a selection of instruments.

Sessions fourteen and fifteen:

Design and technology

Discuss with the class what material would make the best boat and what they think they would need to do to make sure that their boat is water tight.

Ask groups of children to make boats that will be strong enough to hold models of the Owl and the Pussy Cat, and which will float without sinking for a given period of time such as overnight or all day.

Take photographs of the different stages as the investigation unfolds and encourage children to reflect on how their thinking changes and develops during the exploration and what they think they have learnt. The story of the project can then be collected together into a book with annotated comments from both you and the children, or, presented as a display of the work selected by the children.

No Dinner!
Jessica Souhami

A teaching sequence of 4 to 5 weeks

Learning aims

- To learn more about the themes and structures of traditional tales

- To develop skills and experience in storytelling

- To explore and interpret stories through creative activity, including drama, puppetry and art

- To write with confidence for real purposes and audiences

Links with PNS objectives

- To tell and retell stories, ordering events using story language
- To interpret a text by reading aloud with variety of emphasis
- To make predictions showing an understanding of ideas, events and characters

Key Teaching Approaches

Booktalk

Drama and role-play

Storytelling

Story mapping

Writing in role

Re-enactment through play

Drawing and annotating

Shared writing

Bookmaking

Across the Indian sub-continent, there are many versions of this traditional trickster tale in which good triumphs over evil.

In this version, a frail old woman sets out to visit her grand-daughter who lives on the other side of a thick forest inhabited by fierce and hungry animals. Each one is eager to have her for their dinner. But, the brave old woman wins through with the help of her sharp wits and her grand-daughter's cunning plan. The story is recounted simply in patterned and catchy language with an enjoyable build up of tension. Will the old woman escape being eaten by the many animals who threaten to devour her?

Jessica Souhami has drawn on her skill as a shadow puppeteer in her vibrant illustrations, placing each character and setting against a white background so that they glow with colour.

CD materials

The Bookpower 1 CD contains specific teaching materials for use with *No Dinner!*.

Before beginning this unit of work

Collect together a basket of traditional tales from around the world to use in class and guided reading sessions. Encourage children to select from the collection for their own personal reading. Include stories such as 'The Three Billy Goats Gruff' and 'Hansel and Gretel' which are echoed within *No Dinner!* as well as other versions of the story. Include some of Jessica Souhami's other books such as *The Leopard's Drum* and *Rama and the Demon King*. Read them aloud regularly and talk with the children about their choices and what it is they like about them.

Session one:

Booktalk and the class reading journal

Before starting the book, show the children the cover. You could either do this with the whole class using the interactive whiteboard or in groups using laminated photocopies of the front cover. Ask the children to talk together in twos to share their first thoughts about the story.

What do you think this story might be about? Does the cover make you think of any other stories that you know?

Talk together about these ideas as a whole class and list the ideas so that they can be returned to later. Have a Big Book already made up for use as a class reading journal that you can add to as you work with *No Dinner!*

Read aloud the first three pages of the story until just before the old woman's first meeting with the wolf. Ask children to work in pairs to decide how they think this sentence might end and to write it down on a post-it note. Invite the class to share some of their finished sentences before pinning them all up to return to next time.

Session two:

Reading aloud and prediction

Ask the children what they can remember about the story so far, referring to their previous predictions to help recall and anticipate the story. Read aloud from the beginning of the story to the point where the old woman reaches her granddaughter's house. As a class, discuss what they think will happen in the next part of the story and ask if it reminds them of any other stories. Using shared writing record this prediction in the class reading journal.

Read aloud to the end of the book.

Session three:

Shared reading

Make an enlarged version of the story for the class to read aloud together. Before beginning, focus on the text printed in bold and rehearse these parts together. Draw the children's attention to the exclamation and speech marks and ask why the author used them. Does it make it easier to read the story well?

Divide the class into groups to read in role as the bear, the tiger, the wolf, the old woman, her daughter or along with you as narrator.

Read aloud together with expression!

Freeze-frame

Re-read the story up to the part where the old woman meets the wolf on her way home. Close the book and put the children into pairs to make freeze-frames of the moment. Ask them what their character says and what they are thinking.

Drama and writing in role

Put the children into small groups to act out the whole story as you storytell or read aloud the story. Take photographs of the children in role. Ask the children to write what their own character says into a speech bubble. Make a wall display of the photographs with the speech bubbles and, using shared writing, write captions to tell each part of the story.

Booktalk and text-marking

Re-read the story aloud. Using the 'Tell me' questions, discuss with the class the things they liked or disliked in the book, focusing on the language and how it helps us 'see' the story. Ask for volunteers to act out what the old woman is like.

How do you know what the old woman is like? Which words does the writer use to tell us?

Put the first few pages of the book onto the interactive whiteboard and as a class highlight all the words and phrases that describe what the old woman is like at the beginning of the story.

Re-enactment through play

Role-play
Provide a basket of props containing animal masks or head bands, clothes or pieces of Indian fabric, a stick, and maybe even a pumpkin. Children can use the props to re-enact the story either inside or outside the classroom.

Storyprops

As a guided reading activity, make a set of magnetic or stick props with the children. Encourage the children to look at and talk about the pictures as they work.

Place the props in the book area along with a tape or CD version of the story. Provide the story told in community languages where possible.

Session eight:

Story maps

As a class, draw a story map of the old woman's journey to her grand-daughter's. Start from the old woman's house and refer to the book and its pictures to guide making the map. Ask pairs of children to create their own story maps, drawing and labelling the places the old woman passes and the animals she meets on her journey. Suggest the children annotate their maps using speech and thought bubbles, drawing on the language of the story.

Session nine:

Storytelling

Make a storytelling circle with you retelling the old woman's story as the narrator while children come into the middle to act out the story. Write out the statements and questions of the animals and the replies of the old woman as prompts for the children to perform together as shared reading. Then pass the story around the circle from child to child.

Session ten:

Shared writing

Write a postcard as if you were the grand-daughter writing to the old woman. Read it out loud to the class.

What do the children think the old woman would write to her grand-daughter when she arrived home?

Using shared writing, write this postcard together as if written by the old woman. Children can go on to write their own postcards. Suggest some children send text messages or emails.

In guided writing, make a track game of the story which starts and finishes at the old woman's house. Mark the track every three or four spaces with the word 'Boo!' or 'The old woman'.

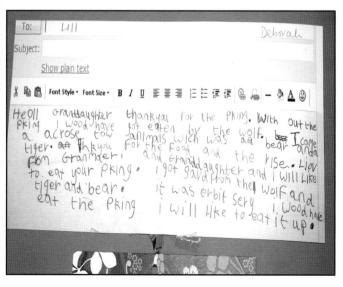

Make a set of 'Boo!' cards. On the back of each of these ask children to choose and write a sentence from the text which is about the animals in the story. Make a set of 'old woman' cards. On the back of each of these children should write a sentence that is taken from the rest of the story. As shared writing, write the instructions for playing the game. Then play the game in small groups with children picking up and reading aloud the cards as they land on them.

Session eleven:

Mapping visits to relatives or friends

Talk with the class about how the old woman goes to visit her grand-daughter who lives on the other side of the forest.

Ask the children if they ever make long journeys to visit relatives or friends.

Plot together some of the journeys children have made, using appropriate maps where possible. Ask the children to draw and annotate their own map of such a journey.

Session twelve:

ICT and shared writing

Prepare a Powerpoint containing some of the photographs of the children in role as each of the animals and the phrases 'Boo!' and 'Old woman, I'm going to eat you up!' Ask the class to make suggestions as to which fonts, size and colours are most effective.

Discuss with the class what other animals the old woman might meet on her journey. What would they say to the old woman?

Using shared writing, create a page for each new animal. Illustrate these with either imported images or scan in children's drawings.

Session thirteen:

Responding to illustration and booktalk

Before beginning this session, put together a collection of books and images related to the forests of the Indian sub-continent and select some websites to click onto.

Re-read the story. Divide the children into small groups and ask them to look at the pictures from the book and discuss where they think the story is set.

Is it in the town or the country?
What's the weather like there? How do you know?
Is it set in the past, present or future?
What clues are there?

Collect the different groups' ideas in the class reading journal and make a list of the questions generated by the children about the setting. Discuss where they can find the answers to their questions.

Put children into pairs to browse and find out more about what this part of the world is like using the weblinks already selected, or working in groups with sets of information texts.

Session fourteen:

Painting

Children go on to paint large pictures of the Indian landscape using a choice of media such as watercolour, powder paint or pastels.

Sessions fifteen, sixteen and seventeen:

Bookmaking

As a class, map out the main events of the story. Think of a chapter title for each one of these and give the different chapters to individual children to write and illustrate. Less confident writers could write theirs as a pair or group in guided writing. When they are finished children can

illustrate the books delicately with a collage of tissue in the style of the original. Bind each sequence together into a complete book and put the finished books into the book corner. Some children will also enjoy writing and publishing their own versions of the story.

Session eighteen:

Debate and argument

Discuss with the children why they think the book is called *No Dinner!*
Have they ever been hungry themselves?
Do they think it's right for the animals to try to eat the old woman?

After the old woman has stayed with her grand-daughter we are told she is 'nice and fat'. Discuss with the children whether they think this is a good thing.
Why do they think the old woman thinks it is a good thing?

Sessions nineteen and twenty:

Performing with shadow puppets

Put the children into groups to make shadow puppets of all the characters and places including the forest itself. Re-enact the story against a screen in front of a strong light. Listen together to some examples of Indian music and choose some that the children feel will convey the right atmosphere.

Give each group time to rehearse their play before presenting it in a final performance in assembly or for another class to enjoy. Children will also enjoy making posters or writing a programme to accompany the show.

The Story Tree
Retold by Hugh Lupton

A teaching sequence of 4 to 5 weeks

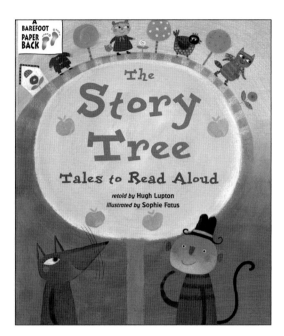

Learning aims

- To develop opinions and personal preferences through booktalk and reading choices

- To understand more about story structure through visualising and mapping

- To explore how stories are told in different ways

- To explore and interpret stories through creative activity, including drama, storytelling, song-writing and art

This is a collection of seven folktales from around the world retold by a gifted storyteller. Versions of some of the stories such as 'The Three Billy Goats Gruff' and 'The Little Red Hen' will be familiar to most children while others such as 'The Blue Coat' may be less so.

The two stories selected to work with are: 'The Sweetest Song', an African-American story in which a little girl goes out to pick flowers, and, absorbed in what she is doing, soon wanders off deep into the forest. She has to think fast to get away from the wolf she meets there.

'Little Cock Feather-Frock' is a tale from Russia about a cat, a blackbird, and a rooster. While the cat and blackbird are out at work, a cunning fox tries to steal the rooster and the cat and blackbird have to work hard to thwart his plans and save their friend.

However, teachers will want to read and re-read all the stories from this collection to their classes and encourage children to discover their own personal favourites.

Sophie Fatus' bright and detailed illustrations intertwine with the text on the page to bring the story to life

Links with PNS objectives

- To retell stories, ordering events using story language
- To explore themes and characters through improvisation and role-play
- To make predictions showing an understanding of ideas, events and characters

Key Teaching Approaches

Visualising

Drama and role-play

Booktalk

Story mapping

Shared writing

Storytelling

Writing in role

Bookmaking

Before beginning this unit of work:

Make a collection of other folktales that feature a clever hero or heroine, a wolf, or a foolish animal. Display the books in an inviting and accessible way. Make a point of regularly browsing this collection with the class, pulling out favourites to read aloud and talk about together. Encourage children to dip into the books as much as possible in independent and shared reading times. You might also read and discuss a story in guided reading.

Add a map of the world to the display so that each story can be plotted onto its country of origin as you read it together, some children might also enjoy finding out a little more about the country that each story originates from.
Prepare a Big Book for use as a class reading journal. This can be added to as each story is read together.

The Sweetest Song
An African-American Story

Session one:

Visualising

Tell the children you are going to read them a story called 'The Sweetest Song' and ask them what a story with a title such as this one might be about.
What do you think this story might be about?
What sort of song is a sweet song?
Do you know any songs that you might describe like this?

Storytell the story to the class as far as the point when Little Daughter starts to sing. Do this without revealing the pictures.
Tell the children that you want them to listen to the beginning of the story carefully and to watch the story in their mind's eye. Then ask them:

What sort of place do you see in your head?
What do you think's going to happen next?
What sort of story do you think this is?

Make a list of all the children's ideas on a flip chart.
In pairs or as individuals, children should now draw the setting for the story using pastels.

Session two:

Drama, role-play and freeze-framing

Read aloud the next paragraph in which the wolf silently arrives. Put the children into pairs to act out what happens in this paragraph, freezing and holding the final moment as if it was a photograph.

Split the class into two groups to show their work in turn, with one half acting it out while the observing group questions individuals about what they are thinking.

Number all the children as number 1s and number 2s. 1s are to be The Wolf and 2s are Little Daughter. Each writes what their character is thinking into a pre-prepared speech bubble. Ask them to read these to a different Wolf or Little Daughter before sharing some of them together as a class and discussing similarities in their ideas.

Pin the speech bubbles up and read to the end of the story.

Session three:

Booktalk and the class reading journal

Using the 'Tell me' questions discuss the children's first responses to the story.

What did you like about the story?
Were there things you didn't like?
Were there things that puzzled you?

Write a first entry as a class into the class reading journal using shared writing.

Sessions four and five:

Drama, role-play and story mapping

Retell the story with the children in role. Put the class into two groups with half the class acting as The Wolf and half becoming Little Daughter. This activity will need some space and benefit from taking place in the hall or somewhere similar.
Collect the children back together as a class and map out the skeleton of the plot onto the flip chart.
Children go on to work in pairs using large sheets of paper to draw and illustrate a story map of the story. Suggest children add speech and thought bubbles and annotate their maps where appropriate with some of the language from the story.

Children might also write the beginning of the story together.

When the maps are finished, children can use them as prompts to help tell the story to others in the class or to children in another class or in assembly. They can also use their maps as a first re-working for writing their own narrative version of the story.

Another way to do this would be to paint and collage a bigger version for the wall with individual children or pairs of children working on different parts of the story.

Session six:

Drama, role-play and hot-seating

Suggest the class present the story as the six o'clock news, inviting characters from the story to come along to be interviewed. These might include Little Daughter's mum and dad as well as The Wolf itself. The class will need to think together about the sorts of questions that a reporter might ask before the characters arrive. Choose one child to stand in as the presenter of the show.

Session seven:

Publishing

Confident users of ICT could film this performance while other children could pose as photographers and take photographs. Children will enjoy turning this into a newspaper report using a programme such as Publisher.

Sessions eight and nine:

Writing in role and bookmaking

Children can now write the story in role as either The Wolf or Little Daughter and present it as a pop-up book with careful illustrations.

The Sweetest Song

One sunny day I heard a girl sing a song "Traiy bla, Traiy bla, cum qua kimo" and I told the girl "Can you sing that song again and the girl sang that song again. I closed my eyes and smiled and then the girl crept back to the gate.

Harry Shepherd

Session ten:

Debate and argument

Ask the class what they think of the way Little Daughter behaved. Do they think she was naughty? Do they think she was clever to trick the wolf in the way that she does? Capture children's views of this within the class reading journal.

Sessions eleven and twelve:

Shared writing

Talk with the children again about what they think the title of the book means.

What do you think 'a sweet song' would be like?

List their ideas onto a flip chart before writing a song together as a piece of shared writing. A possible way to begin would be to build on from Little Daughter's song, using it as a beginning or as a refrain. Use instruments to play along with it, and make it into a poster-size song sheet for class singing. Some children might also like to write and then record their own songs. These could be saved into a Powerpoint and illustrated using photographs of the drama or the children's own scanned drawings.

Little Cock Feather-Frock
A Russian Tale

Booktalk and word-collecting

Read the story aloud to the point where Foxy finally succeeds in his mission and the cat and blackbird return home to find the cockerel gone with only a trail of footprints to help.
Using the 'Tell me' questions, talk with the children about the story so far.

Is there anything you particularly like?
Is there anything you don't like?
Does anything puzzle you?
What do you think is going to happen next?

If no one mentions the language of the story draw attention to it yourself. You can do this by modelling a comment such as 'One of the things that I particularly like about this story is the name the storyteller gives the cockerel'. Read the story aloud to the end.

Make a collection of any words or phrases from the story that children have remembered in particular, using shared writing to write them down. This will provide an opportunity to discuss the pictures that the language creates for individual children in their heads and talk about the ways that the author does this through their choice of vocabulary and other aspects of language usage such as rhyme, rhythm, or alliteration.

Visualising

As a class write the cast list for the story.
What do the children think each character is like?
Ask each of them to choose a character from the story and describe what they are like to a partner.
Children can now go on to draw them.
Alternatively, children can work in pairs with one child describing the character for the other child to draw.

Booktalk and the class reading journal

Talk again with the children about the parts of the story that they particularly liked and enjoyed, re-reading parts of the original story and referring back to the original predictions that they made.

Did this story remind you of any others that you know?

Using shared writing, write the children's responses into the class reading journal.
Suggest to the children that some of them might like to add their own comments later.

Storytelling

Before this session begins write the repeated chants of the story out onto large sheets of paper. These will form the text for a shared reading of the story.
Put the children into four character groups - cat, cockerel, blackbird, old foxy.
Storytell the story and ask the children to join in reading the chants in role.

Storytelling and role-play

Sit the children in a storytelling circle to 'pass the story around'. Stop at important parts of the story, asking children to go into the middle of the circle to act them out. You might use the 'clack-click' of the story to mark these points, or mark them with a musical instrument.

Writing in role and bookmaking

Using shared writing, write the very beginning of the story together as a class group. This section can then be photocopied and given to children to stick into their individual books before they go on to write the story in role as one of the animals. When they are finished, children should illustrate their books and share them with the class before placing them in the book corner for everyone to enjoy.

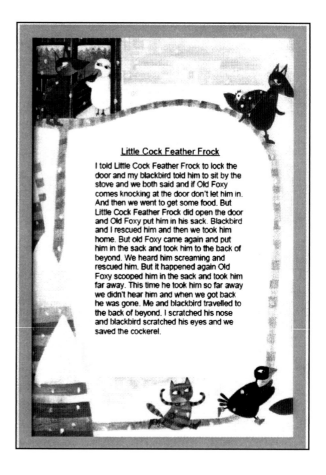

Little Cock Feather Frock

I told Little Cock Feather Frock to lock the door and my blackbird told him to sit by the stove and we both said and if Old Foxy comes knocking at the door don't let him in. And then we went to get some food. But Little Cock Feather Frock did open the door and Old Foxy put him in his sack. Blackbird and I rescued him and then we took him home. But old Foxy came again and put him in the sack and took him to the back of beyond. We heard him screaming and rescued him. But It happened again Old Foxy scooped him in the sack and took him far away. This time he took him so far away we didn't hear him and when we got back he was gone. Me and blackbird travelled to the back of beyond. I scratched his nose and blackbird scratched his eyes and we saved the cockerel.

Jamela's Dress
Niki Daly

A teaching sequence of 3 to 4 weeks

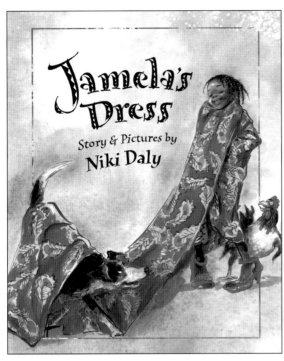

Learning aims

- To discuss issues raised by the story and readers' responses to characters and events

- To develop an understanding of another cultural and geographical setting

- To explore and investigate language

Links with PNS objectives

- To visualise and comment on events, characters and ideas, making imaginative links to own experiences
- To find and use new and interesting words and phrases, including story language
- To explore familiar themes and characters through improvisation and role-play
- To write chronological and non-chronological texts using simple structures

Jamela so loves the beautiful material that her mother has bought to make a dress to attend a wedding that she wraps it around herself and, oblivious to how dirty and torn it is becoming, she parades around the South African township where she lives. It could be a disaster but rescue comes in the shape of prize money won by a neighbour who takes a photograph of the incident and so turns it into a triumph.

This is a warm and humorous story with universal appeal. It gives a strong sense of both the geography and the culture of its setting enabling readers to feel that they could walk down the street alongside Jamela herself.

Jamela's Dress is the first of several books starring the irrepressible Jamela by the South African author/illustrator Niki Daly whose work is distinguished by his ability to impart a child's eye view of the world. The rhythmic musical language perfectly complements the bold pictures.

Key Teaching Approaches

Visualising

Shared writing

Re-enactment through play

Drama and role-play

Responding to illustration

Word collections

Introduction

Introduce *Jamela's Dress* to the class by first asking them to talk together about the illustration on the front cover. You could either do this with the whole class, using the interactive whiteboard or in groups using laminated photocopies. Ask the children to talk together in twos about their first responses.

What do you think this story might be about?
What do you think Jamela is like?
Have you read any other Jamela stories?

Talk about these first ideas as a whole class before reading the first five pages of the story. Ask the children to discuss in pairs if they have ever had to wear something special for a special event such as a wedding or a naming celebration. Ask some children to talk about their experience with the class and collect them together into the class reading journal or onto a flip chart to return to later.

Ask the class what they think will happen next.

Visualising

Look again at the pictures of Jamela wrapped in the material.

Ask the class what they think Jamela is thinking.

Get the children to close their eyes and read the passage starting, 'A warm breeze . . .' and ending with '. . . wrapped around her into a dress.' Ask the children to describe how the fabric feels and looks.

How do they think Jamela feels with the fabric wrapped around her?

Put children into pairs to draw an outline of Jamela wrapped in the material. Outside the outline they should write words to describe the fabric, and inside the outline record what she is thinking and feeling.

Shared writing and reading

Ask the children to share their annotated drawings with a partner. Ask them as a pair to choose words or phrases which they particularly like. Bring the class back together again and write a list of these choices using a flip chart or interactive white-board.

Write a shared list poem about the fabric and how Jamela feels about it, taking turns to choose from the original list. Keep reading and re-reading the poem as it builds.

Are there any lines or phrases that they would like to repeat?

When it is finished read the poem out loud again with the children.

How does it sound? Which is their favourite part?

Once the children's final suggestions have been incorporated into the poem they should illustrate their own copy.

Re-enactment through play

Create a clothes and fabric shop in the role-play area. Include fabric and clothes for the children to wear, or to buy and sell. Capitalise on the literacy opportunities that the role-play presents such as the writing of labels, prices, shopping lists, and receipts.

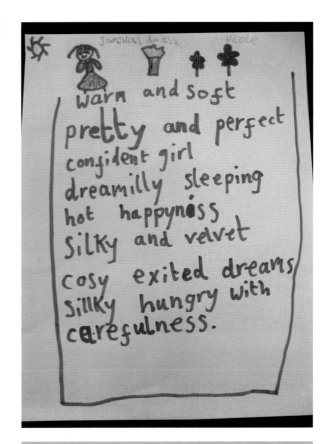

Drama and role-play

Read aloud the whole story to the end. Now work together as a whole class with everybody taking each role in turn to act out the street scene. Ask children to work in groups to create a freeze-frame of the scene in the street just before the crash, when people are shouting out 'Hi, beautiful' and 'Kwela Jamela, African Queen'.

Give the children some time to practice what they will do and say before asking each group in turn to show the class their work. Touch each character in turn and ask them to voice their thoughts in role. Write these onto thought bubbles and place them around a photocopy of the picture in the class reading journal.

Session six:

Drama and role-play

Look together at the double page spread where Mama and Thelma are upset, and re-read these pages aloud.

How is everybody feeling?

Put the children into two groups to create a 'conscience alley' to articulate these thoughts. The children on one side are going to offer Jamela's thoughts/feelings while the other side are going to say what Mama and the aunties are thinking. Choose a child to walk through the alley.

'Even Jamela was cross with Jamela.'

Ask the children to discuss this idea.

What do they think it means ?
Have they ever been cross with themselves? Did those feelings make them change their behaviour?

Session seven:

Investigating language

Look at the picture of Archie holding up a copy of the newspaper which contains the photograph he took of Jamela. The headline in the newspaper is 'Kwela Jamela African Queen' which the children are singing. Talk with the class about the ways in which Kwela and Jamela rhyme. Put them into pairs to create rhymes and songs for their own names.

Session eight:

Information writing

Provide a mock-up of a newspaper page which children can use to 'put themselves in the news' using a photograph or drawing of themselves and adding their own headlines. Display them all alongside the Jamela story collection.

Responding to illustration

Look again at the photograph of Jamela and her family all dressed up for the wedding.

Have they ever been to a wedding? What sort of clothes did everybody wear? Can they think of other occasions when people wear special clothes?

Ask children to bring photographs or examples from home of the clothes they and their families wear for these special occasions. Make a display and ask children and parents to write a caption to explain their exhibit.

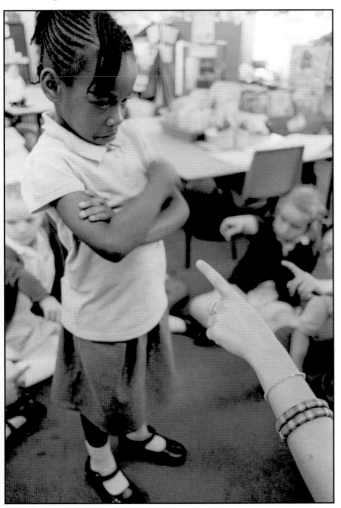

Word collections

Starting with *Enkosi kakhulu* make a collection of words meaning 'Thank you very much'. Ask the children to bring in words from any other languages and script that also mean 'thank you very much'. Begin a class display, adding to it as more examples are brought in from home. Encourage children to use them as part of the classroom language repertoire.

Investigating the setting

Re-read the story. In pairs ask the children to look at different pictures from the text and to be 'reading detectives', talking together to find clues to identify where the story is set.

What does the book tell you about how the place looks?
What do you think it would be like to live there?
How do you know?
Is the story set in the past or present?
How do you know?

Record the children's ideas into the class reading journal. Make a list of any questions generated by the children about the setting, and discuss with the class where they can find answers to their questions.

Information writing: researching South Africa

Show the children where South Africa is in the world using a large world map or the interactive whiteboard. Talk with the children about what they already know about what South Africa is like; some children may have personal or family experience of the country, or with other places in Africa, to share.

Enlarge a map of South Africa so that the names of the towns can be seen clearly.

Put the children into research groups to find out five interesting things about South Africa within a particular theme such as homes, food, weather, music or city life. Each group should be given a small collection of information books and resources such as photographs. Suggest they

collect each new fact by drawing or writing it onto a post-it note. They can then work as a group to make an illustrated poster of their findings. More experienced writers can go on to write their own information books.

Drawing and illustrating

Music is a defining part of South African life. Ask the children to shut their eyes while you play some southern African music. Talk with them about how it makes them feel, the sorts of colours or sounds it communicates, and the sorts of pictures that it creates for them in their mind's eye.

Suggest children work in pairs or as individuals to paint a picture as if they were Jamela looking out of her bedroom window.

Aaaarrgghh, Spider!
Lydia Monks

Spider's greatest wish is to be a family pet but despite showing the family how talented she is at dancing, feeding and washing, all they do is scream, "Aaaarrgghh, SPIDER!" and throw her outside.

It is not until she makes beautiful sparkly webs in the garden that the family relents - much to the delight of the spider whose story this is. However a clever and unexpected twist at the end leads us all to think again.

This book is a funny, enjoyable and memorable read that will soon have the class convulsed in giggles of shared and horrified pleasure.
It also offers the opportunity to talk together about more serious themes of tolerance and misunderstanding and to explore the basis for one of humankind's most common phobias.

A teaching sequence of 3 to 4 weeks

Learning aims

- To explore, develop and sustain ideas through talk, listening to and responding to others' contributions

- To empathise and engage with characters through role-play and writing

- To explore and interpret stories through creative activity, including drama, storytelling, poetry and art

- To enlarge responses to the ideas and themes of the book through purposeful information reading and writing

Links with PNS objectives

- To explore relevant themes and characters through improvisation and role-play
- To make predictions showing an understanding of ideas, events and characters
- To visualise and comment on events, characters and ideas, making imaginative links to own experiences
- To distinguish fiction and non-fiction texts and the different purposes for reading them

Key Teaching Approaches

Responding to illustration

Drawing and annotating

Drama and role-play

Shared writing

Re-enactment through play

Debate and argument

Bookmaking

Before beginning this unit of work:

Make a display about spiders for children to
browse together. Include photographs and other
images of spiders and their webs, collections of
poetry and stories as well as models and
storyprops for children to re-enact the story with.
Place a variety of resources nearby such as
magnifying glasses and clipboards. Encourage
children to use these to draw or write about
anything of interest that they find out and to
write down questions that they want answering.
Make a regular time for children to talk to the
class about their discoveries and to raise the
questions they have.

Session one:

Introducing the book

Begin by talking with the children about their
pets.

Do they have any? Are there pets that they would
like to have if only their parents would allow it?
What reasons do their parents give them for why
they aren't allowed to have certain pets?

Ask children what they think would happen if they
asked to have a spider for a pet. Would they like
it? Would the members of their family like it?
What sorts of things do people they know say
about spiders?

On a flip chart jot these down in a list as you talk together, starting with:
Spiders are…..

You could finish by adding one of your own-
'Aaaarrgghh, Spider!'

Pin up this list to refer back to later.

Session two:

Responding to illustration, class reading journal

Show the children the initial picture from the book on the interactive whiteboard but turn it the right way up and cover over the text. Talk together with the children about anything they notice before zooming the picture round to focus in on the spider.
Read the story aloud to the end.

Talk with children about their initial responses to this story.

What did you like about it?
What didn't you like?
What did you think about the ending?

Scribe their comments into a class reading journal.

Session three:

Drawing

Ask the children:

What would the world look like if you were a spider?

Suggest children draw 'the spider's eye view' of their bedroom or another room in their house.

Session four:

Reading in role and freeze-framing

Before this session you will need to enlarge the text so that it is big enough for shared class reading. You might, for example, make an electronic copy or you might rewrite it as a Big Book. Children will enjoy illustrating this Big Book version as they get to know the book better.

Read the story in parts, with half the class reading the part of the spider and half the class reading in role as the different members of the family.
Act out the story with everybody taking all the parts first before giving individuals specific roles and acting it out again.

Ask the children to make a freeze-frame of the living room scene where the spider tries dancing. Go round the family group asking each family member in turn to say what they are thinking

Children can go on to write their own thought bubbles for the scene.

Session five:

Drawing and annotating

What are spiders like?

With the children's help, draw a large spider on a flip chart or interactive whiteboard. Around the outside of the drawing write everything the children already know about spiders, and inside the drawing write all the questions they want to find answers to. (For example, they might ask, 'What do spiders eat? What are baby spiders like? Do all spiders make webs?')

Children will also be able to draw on this chart as a word bank for their own independent writing.

Session six:

Spider hunt

Equipped with magnifying glasses, paper and crayons and cameras take the children on a spider hunt in the playground.

What sort of spiders can they find and where do they live? Are they the same as the ones that they might see in the house?

On your return use the internet to find out more and to look more closely at what spiders are like.

Session seven:

Researching spiders

What do we want to find out about spiders?

Ask the class to look again at the chart that they made in session five and decide which questions they are most interested in finding answers for. Write each of these questions onto a large poster-sized piece of paper. Children should now work in groups to research individual questions, using a variety of information books and resources. Provide post-it notes for them to use to write or draw what they discover, these can easily be collected onto the posters. When they have finished, work with each group to sort and discuss what they have found out. Groups can then report back their findings to the rest of the class in turn.

Session eight:

Shared information writing

Using shared writing write a class Big Book about spiders, adding a new page each day about something that the children have observed or found out. Children can illustrate each page using a variety of media. More experienced writers could go on to write their own information books using pre-prepared books. When finished, these should be shared with the class and put into the book corner for everyone to enjoy.

Spider webs

Spiders spin their webs early in the morning.
Spiders use their spinnerets to make very strong webs.
They catch flies in their sticky webs.

Session nine:

Book corner

Turn the book corner into a spider's web. Involve the children in setting it up. You might construct a vast spider's web to hang at the front or over the top. Place a spider toy inside for children to read with and have a 'Spider's book of the week' display to feature other spider stories, for example, those of Anancy or Spiderman.

Session ten:

Painting and collage

Display some images of spider webs onto the interactive whiteboard to show the children how the spider builds one.

Children can experiment to construct a spider's web using silver paint or crayon on black paper or they can create one from collage materials.

Children could make spiders and hang them around the classroom to create the final living room scene.

We like spiders because....	We don't like spiders because....

Debate and argument

Talk with the children about what they now know about spiders and their role in the food-chain.

Discuss questions such as:

Are spiders good or bad?
Should people be more willing to have them in their homes?

Collect children's thoughts together in a comparison chart.

Re-enactment through play

With the children's help, set up the role-play area as Spiderman's office, providing pieces of fabric for capes. Involve the children in assembling it and in making anything that they might need to help the play along. This will provide lots of reasons for children to write as they make materials such as labels, notices, or leaflets. Include a rich range of resources such as different writing materials and tools.

Small world play
Create a garden in a builder's tray using a variety of twig, leaf and bark material and add an assortment of toy spiders and insects for children to use to make up their own stories and games. Alternatively make a story box with the children.

Bookmaking

Make individual books within which children can draw and write their own versions of *Aaaarrgghh, Spider!*. Show children how to draw the character of the spider and attach it by a ribbon to the book so that they can move it in and out of the story as they read their work to each other.

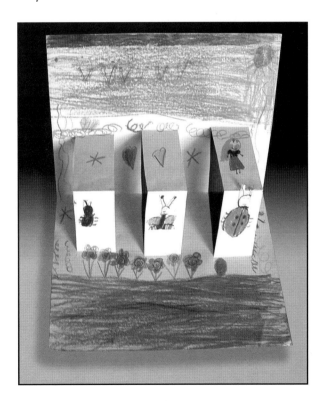

Shared poetry writing

As a class, re-read the list that was written at the beginning of the project and talk with the children about how they now feel about spiders and whether they agree with these comments.
Using a flip chart and with you scribing to help shape their ideas, write the first verse of a poem together using an open structure such as the following:

When people see spiders they...

leading to the refrain...

How do you think a spider feels?
How do you think a spider feels?

Give everybody a small folded piece of paper with 'But I think...' on the outside and ask them to finish the sentence inside.

Collect the class together again to share each other's ideas. Then write a second verse together. Illustrate and display this poem in the book corner.

Drama and role-play, shared writing

Look again at the final pages of the story and talk with the children about what they think would happen next to the spider and its friends. They will probably decide that they would all need to look for a new home!

In drama, ask the children to create a garden scene with all the children in role as an insect or animal that already lives there.

What do you think these animals would say to the spider if it came to them looking for a new home?

Put the children into groups as different minibeasts and ask them to improvise a response to the spider's request, with you acting as scribe to help them shape their work into a play for performance as an assembly or to another class.

Bookmaking

Provide opportunities for children to write their own versions of the story under the title 'The spider who wanted a home'.

Spiders

Spiders, spiders, spiders,
Big, hairy, black spiders.
Crawling, tickling, spinning spiders,
Patterned, sparkling webs.
Sticky webs, catching flies
Spiders, spiders, spiders.

Spiders, spiders, spiders,
In the corner, on the tree,
Under the chair, in the bath,
Under my bed, in my loft.
Spiders, spiders everywhere.
Spiders, spiders, spiders.

Aaaargh!

spider

The homeless butterfly
by Maddy
Once upon a time there was a very pretty butterfly. She was called charlotte. She had absolutely splendid wings, but she had no home.

One day she went to find a home. Soon she came to a small heap of twigs. "What lives here?" asked charlotte.

"I DO" said a cross soldier ant "NOW YOU JUST SHOO OFF! GET OUT! GO!"
So away went Charlotte!

Soon she came to a bush.
" Please can I live with you?" asked Charlotte, to a little ladybird that she had found there.
" I'd love you to" said the ladybird "but I'm sorry-there is no room."
So away went Charlotte!
Soon she alighted on a green leaf.
Soon Charlotte saw a spider.
'Please can I live with you?' asked Charlotte.
'I'd love you to', said the spider 'because I am lonely and I need some nice brightly coloured wings in the house with me!
But I am so sorry there is a problem. The problem is that there's no room.'

So Charlotte went on her way

Where the Wild Things Are
Maurice Sendak

A teaching sequence of 3 weeks

Learning aims

- To talk confidently about a book using prediction, asking questions, expressing opinions

- To discuss the themes and issues that arise enabling children to make connections with their own lives

- To respond to illustration

- To develop creative responses to a book through play, drawing, talk, writing, music and art

Max dresses up in his wolf suit one evening and makes mischief of one kind and another. As a result, he is sent to bed by his mother without any supper. Once in his room, a mysterious, wild forest grows and Max journeys off to the land of the Wild Things. These are fearsome-looking monsters who roar their terrible roars, gnash their terrible teeth, roll their terrible eyes and show their terrible claws until Max conquers them with a bold stare and is made the King of all Wild Things. Now the rumpus begins. Max and the Wild Things whoop and hurl around to their hearts' content. However, Max is lonely and homesick and so returns home to his bedroom. Here he finds his supper waiting for him ... "And it was still hot."

This is a classic tale which explores contradictory emotions of anger and love accompanied by forgiveness.

Maurice Sendak's illustrations explore the power of the imagination to transform.

Links with PNS objectives

- To retell stories, ordering events using story language
- To read more challenging texts
- To visualise and comment on events, characters and ideas, making imaginative links to own experience
- To use key features of narrative, creating chronological and non-chronological texts on paper and screen

Key Teaching Approaches

Booktalk

Drama and role-play

Story mapping

Re-enactment through play

Responding to illustration

Bookmaking

Debate and argument

Reading aloud and booktalk

Read the story straight through to the class. Then re-read it, returning to particular pages to discuss and leisurely explore the story and the pictures so that all the children know it quite well.

Read it again, this time encouraging children to join in the words, so that they remember parts of the language clearly.

Drama and role-play, visualising

Act out the story with you as narrator and all the children taking the role of everything as you move through the story. Stop at various points to help the children to enter this fictional world more completely by asking them to visualise where they are. You might for example ask them to imagine that they are on the island and to think what they can see.

What can you see if you look straight ahead?
What would you see if you turned around?
What can you feel under your feet?

Ask children to talk with a partner about their idea of what the island is like. Children can now paint a picture of the land where the Wild Things live.

Story mapping

Put the children into pairs to create a map of the story on large pieces of paper. Encourage them to annotate it with any phrases from the story that they can recall. When they are finished 'pass the story around' with children using their maps to help them with the retelling.

Performing the story

Working first as individuals and then in groups, improvise the rumpus with one child in role as Max to start and finish it. Children could compose their own music to accompany the performance using pitched or unpitched percussion.

Re-enactment through play

Role-play area
Suggest to the class that they turn the role-play area into either the boat that Max used on his journey, or the land where the Wild Things live. Discuss with them what they think each of these places would be like and decide together what sort of props they might make. Capture their ideas as a list. Children can then check these off as they complete each task as well as adding any other ideas they might have as they create the role-play area.

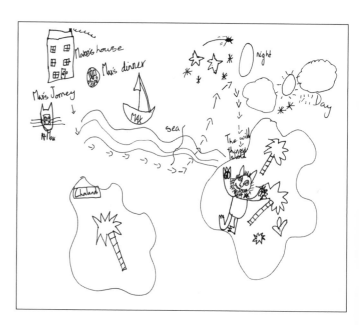

Both scenarios will also present ample opportunities for a variety of writing such as posters, maps, a captain's log, messages in a bottle, treasure maps, notices and labels. You might plan for some of these as teacher-led activities working with the class or group in shared or guided writing.

Storyprops

Invite a group of children to make a set of storyprops which they can use to replay the story. Set up a lamp and screen between which they can create a shadow play of the rumpus.

Story box

Suggest groups of children make their own Wild Things story boxes and use them to help retell the story to their friends or to younger children in another class.

Continue the theme of Max's journey across all areas of provision within the classroom. Examples could include placing a model boat and collection of sea monsters in the water tray or creating the land where the Wild Things are in the sand tray using twigs, bits of moss and a variety of small toys and other interesting objects.

Sessions six and seven:

Responding to illustration and poetry writing

Using laminated pictures of some of the illustrations, put the children into small groups to talk together about what they see and to discuss the ideas and feelings that they provoke. You might, for example, choose the scenes in Max's bedroom when the forest grows, the wild rumpus or the moment after the rumpus when Max wants to be where he is 'loved best of all'. Bring the group back together to talk about their responses, and on a flipchart make a list of the words or phrases which they use. With the help of the class shape these into a poem, choosing the words that convey the mood of the pictures most strongly.

The children can go on to draw their own monster-sized Wild Things in the spirit of the originals using pastels, crayon or paint. Pin these up to create a wall frieze and, as a class, compile a word bank of words to describe them, displaying these around the frieze of pictures.

Booktalk

Talk together as a class about the characters and themes of the story and where possible encourage children to make links with their own experience.

How did this story make you feel?
Does this story remind you of anything that has happened to you?
How was Max feeling?
How was Max's mum feeling?
What sorts of things do you do when you are naughty?

Ask children to write a sentence each about what they like most about the story and why.

Shared writing

Using a flip chart or interactive whiteboard and with you scribing the words composed by the class, re-write the story together. As you scribe talk together about the language and the shape of the story. Write the story in episodes over more than one session; this will enable you to review what you have written and to change and add to it. When it is finished, illustrate each section and bind the whole together to make a Big Book version.

Make individual books for children to use to write their own versions of the story. These can be kept in the writing area or placed alongside any of the story making activities such as the story box. Once the books are finished these should be read to the rest of the group and put with the display.

ICT and bookmaking

Make a multimedia version of the story using Powerpoint by importing photographs of the children's artwork and adding or recording the children's retelling. Alternatively you could use software such as 2simple to animate.

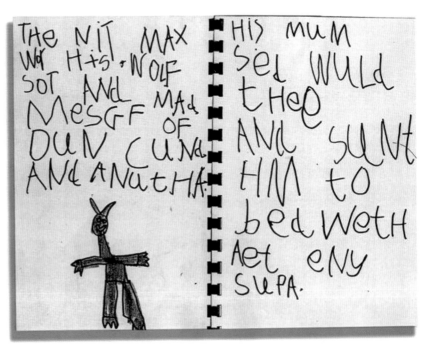

Session thirteen:

Debate and argument

Ask the children how long they thought the story took to happen and whether they thought it really happened. What makes them think that? Record their ideas as a comparison chart.

Do you think Max really went to visit the Wild Things?	
Yes! because	No! because
It says he sailed away over almost a year... In the pictures you see the moon change. *I think it was like Doctor Who and he was in another world at the same time*	*The trees grow in his bedroom so I think he's fallen asleep and he's dreaming...* *If it really happened the monsters would eat him up* *His dinner is still hot*

The Snail and the Whale
Julia Donaldson and Axel Scheffler

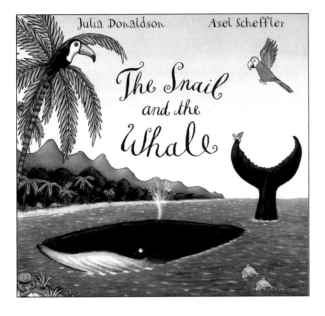

A tiny snail with a lust to travel forges an unlikely friendship with a gentle whale and the two go travelling round the world together. On the way the snail experiences many of the splendours of the natural world meeting icebergs and volcanoes, sharks and penguins. He marvels at its vastness as compared to his own smallness. However, when disaster strikes and the whale is beached in a bay, it is the tiny snail who saves the day.

This simple rhyming book which sweeps the reader along in the style of *This is the house that Jack built* provides opportunities to think together as a class about some important themes; the scope and splendour of the world we live in, how we can all work together to help someone in need, and how even when you are small you can make a big difference.

The illustrations are full of quirky, humorous detail which children will enjoy exploring together and which will provide much for them to talk about.

A teaching sequence of 3 to 4 weeks

Learning aims

- To explore and interpret stories through creative activity, including drama, storytelling and art

- To use both fiction and non-fiction books to find out more about a topic of interest

- To write with confidence for real purposes and audiences

- To write in role to explore different points of view

Links with PNS objectives

- To retell stories, ordering events using story language
- To make predictions showing an understanding of ideas, events and characters
- To visualise and comment on events, characters and ideas, making imaginative links to their own experiences
- To distinguish fiction and non-fiction texts and the different purposes for reading them

Key Teaching Approaches

Responding to illustration

Booktalk

Visualising

Debate and argument

Storytelling

Shared writing

Bookmaking

Re-enactment through play

Writing in role

Before beginning this unit of work:

Make a display of both information and story books about sea snails and whales for children to look at, read and talk about. This will be a useful collection to draw on in reading aloud sessions and when children are choosing for their own independent reading. Provide a variety of resources such as clipboards that children can use to draw or write about anything of interest they find out. Encourage children to write down questions that they want to find answers for by including some pre-drawn speech bubbles. Put aside regular times in the week for children to talk to the class about their discoveries and to discuss the questions they have.

Session one:

Responding to illustration

Look together at the cover of *The Snail and the Whale*. Ask the children to be 'picture detectives' and talk together about what they can see, encouraging them to predict with questions such as:

What sort of story do you think this is?
If the characters were speaking what do you think they would be saying?
Where do you think the creatures are in this picture?

Many of the children may know this book already or be familiar with books by Julia Donaldson and Axel Scheffler.

Read the story aloud stopping first at the point when the whale says 'Come sail with me', and then at the point where the whale gets beached to talk with the children about what they think will happen next. Focus on the snail's decisions and choices, asking:

Should he have gone with the whale? Would you go if you were him?
What would the other snails have said to him?
What could the snail do to help the whale?
Why do you think he was so determined to help?
How do you think the story will end?

Continue to read to the end of the story.

Session two:

Booktalk

Talk with the children about their first responses to the story using the 'Tell me' questions and focussing in particular on their likes and dislikes, exploring any patterns or connections that they have noticed.

Did the story remind you of any other stories that you know?

The children may comment on the theme of friendship, particularly the idea of very big and very small creatures being friends.

Does the way it is written remind you of any other stories or rhymes?

The children may refer to the way in which the author has used the rhythm and patterns of *This is the house that Jack built.*

Session three:

Shared reading

Re-read the story aloud, emphasising its rhyme and rhythm and encouraging the children to join in as much as possible.
Enlarge the first few pages of the book and put groups of children into role to read the parts of the narrator, the whale and the snail. Try out different voices, pitch and volume before performing the whole book out loud.

Session four:

Visualising and painting

Re-read the first few pages up to the point where the whale appears.
Ask the children to close their eyes and to see in their 'mind's eye' the scene the whale describes:

'Who sang to the whale a wonderful song
Of shimmering ice and coral caves
And shooting stars and enormous waves'

Ask children to draw or paint this scene and to write a caption describing it.

Session five:

Debate and argument

Create a wall frieze of the sea with the rock, the snail and the whale. In pairs, ask children to discuss whether they think the snail should stay or go. Bring the class back together again and using shared writing write speech bubbles for the snail and the whale, for example,
'I will take you to places you only dreamt of ....'

Children can go on to make a snail to put on the rock with a speech bubble telling him what they think he should do, for example, 'Stay here it's too dangerous...'

Sessions six and seven:

Drawing and annotating

As a class, map out the key events of the story on a flip chart for the children to draw on in their writing.

Put children into groups to paint their own pictures of one of these events, annotating them with some of the phrases or words that they have recalled from the book. Suggest they include speech bubbles where appropriate. When they have finished, put the class into pairs to tell their part of the story to each other, using the 'This is the...' structure as much as possible.

Storytelling and shared writing

As a class, retell the whole story using the pictures as a guide while you or another adult scribe the children's version.

Read aloud the new version to check that it 'sounds right' and decide with the children whether anything needs to be changed. This will provide an excellent opportunity to talk about what they have written and to check spelling and punctuation.

Display the finished work as a wall story with the paintings and accompanying text pinned alongside each other.

Debate and argument

"'I feel so small', said the snail."
Discuss with the children what they think the snail means since he has always been small. What makes him feel extra small now?
"'I'm too big', said the whale."
What do the children think the whale means? Is he always too big or just this time?

Develop this idea within a circle time activity, asking children to complete the sentences:
'I feel small when . . . .' or 'I feel big when . . . .'

Booktalk, information bookmaking

Select one or two of the information books from the display to browse through with the class.
Look closely together at some of the detail of the pictures or photographs and talk about anything that captures the children's interest.
Discuss with the children their ideas about the relative sizes of the snail and the whale.

Use the internet to find out the size of the humpback whale and what this means when compared to the children themselves and other familiar things such as the classroom or the school hall.
Go out into the playground and pace out the size of a whale.
Some children will enjoy researching and making information books about whales.

Responding to illustration

Put the children into groups to talk around laminated illustrations of one of the places the pair visited. Ask each group to describe what the snail would see and hear when he visited that place, writing their ideas down around the edges of each picture. Go into role as the snail and retell the story with each group telling their own part of the snail's tale.

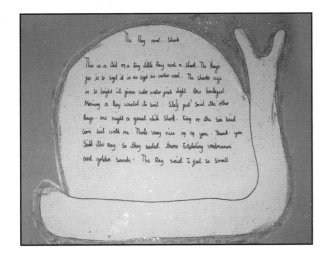

Writing in role

What if the snail had written letters home to the other snails?
What do you think he would have written?

Using shared writing, write the first part of the snail's journey with the children as if it was the snail talking. Children can then go on to write and illustrate their own books in role as the snail. Invite children to share these with the class before placing them in the book corner for everyone to read.

Re-enactment through play

Storyprops
Set up a class puppet theatre using laminated illustrations of the scenes in the story to provide a changing backdrop. Suggest children make storyprops of the main characters and work in groups to tell and retell the story.

Story boxes
Inspired by the main settings in the book, create story boxes with the children. Fill them with a variety of small model animals including some new characters as well as the snail and the whale. Suggest children use them to make the next adventure. Invite children to tell these to the class at storytime. Place a variety of interesting writing materials such as home-made books, postcards and other materials nearby for them to include in their play

Role-play and newspaper reports

Re-read aloud the final section in which the whale gets beached and is then saved by the snail's prompt action. Improvise a cut-out television screen and invite children to role-play a report on the six o'clock news. They might, for example, be the news presenter reporting the event, a reporter at the scene interviewing the snail and the whale, or some of the children and townspeople telling the story of what they saw happen.

Children can go on to write a newspaper report for the local paper about what happened.

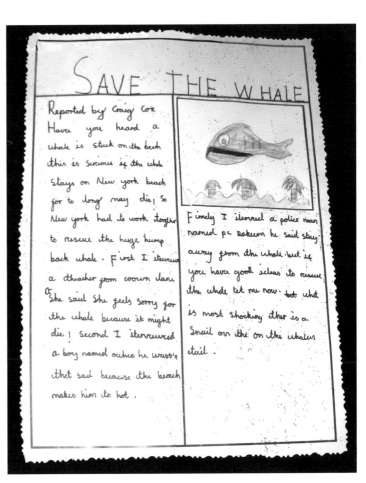

Quentin Blake
Author Study

A teaching sequence of 6 to 7 weeks

This sustained study of Quentin Blake offers readers the opportunity to steep themselves in his work, and to explore what it is that is special and distinctive about the way in which he uses illustration, colour, imagery and language to express and communicate ideas. In this chapter, children's knowledge and appreciation of Quentin Blake will be developed through working in detail with three selected books, exploring how he uses illustration to make meaning and to tell the story. This chapter will focus on the picture books *Cockatoos, Mister Magnolia* and *The Green Ship*. It will be important to introduce children to Quentin Blake's other books so as to provide them with as many opportunities as possible to discover their own favourites among his extensive work.

Learning aims

- To explore and interpret the way Quentin Blake draws and conveys meaning

- To read and engage in depth with a range of books by one illustrator/author

- To encourage children to 'read' illustration critically and closely engage with it

- To develop children's own understanding of the ways in which they can use drawing to communicate meaning

Links with PNS objectives

- To describe and consider the style of one author/illustrator
- To select books for personal reading and give reasons for choices
- To talk confidently about personal responses to a book

Key Teaching Approaches

Booktalk
Class reading journal
Performing poetry
Shared writing
Drama and role-play
Storytelling
Story mapping
Writing in role
Responding to illustration
Bookmaking
Drawing and annotating
Re-enactment through play
Mind-mapping

Before beginning this unit:

Collect together as many examples of Quentin Blake's work as you can. Quentin Blake has illustrated around 300 books and will be well-known to the children for his collaboration with authors such as Roald Dahl and Michael Rosen, as well as for creating his own books as an author and illustrator. Many children will already have established favourites among these and will be familiar with his distinctive style. Put aside time for the children to browse and talk together about this collection on a regular and frequent basis; display the books in an inviting and accessible way and encourage children to dip into them in independent and shared reading times as well as to read and discuss them in guided reading.

Session one:

Introducing Quentin Blake; the class reading journal

Talk to the children about the work that they will be doing for the next few weeks and introduce them to the class reading journal as a way to capture some of the conversations that you will have together.

What do children already know about Quentin Blake?
Do they like his work?

Using shared writing record some of the children's initial comments into the class reading journal.

Using the interactive whiteboard investigate the Quentin Blake website together, www.quentinblake.com, trying out links and reading aloud from it. This is a very informative website which offers many possibilities for children including materials that are designed especially for them. Write anything of interest that you discover onto post-its and collect them onto a large sheet of paper to begin to make the poster 'Who is Quentin Blake?'
Store the links on the computer desktop so that children can work with independence. Ask them to work in pairs, following the links and seeing what they can find out that they might add to the poster.

Booktalk

Which of Quentin Blake's books is your favourite and why?

Invite two or three children to choose a book from the collection to read aloud or talk about to the rest of the group.

What is it that they particularly like about the book?

Ask everyone to browse through the books in the Quentin Blake collection and in pairs to select one book to read and talk about together.
Ask each pair to write a speech bubble to say what they like about their chosen book. These comments can be added to the display either alongside the book itself or pinned onto a scanned picture of the book's cover.

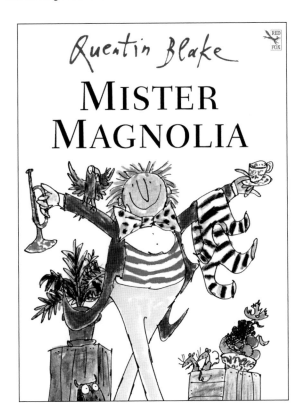

MISTER MAGNOLIA

This is an intoxicating nonsensical poem about the eccentric Mister Magnolia and the fun he gets up to with his menagerie of unusual friends. Throughout there runs the unmissable conundrum of his missing boot which is satisfyingly resolved in the final pages.

Responding to illustration

Introduce the class to the cover picture of *Mister Magnolia* using the interactive whiteboard or a laminated picture.
Who is this person?
What do they think he is like?
Do they think they would like him?
How do they think the illustrator has made them feel like this?
Annotate the picture with the children's comments for revisiting later and paste a copy into the class journal.
Read aloud to the end of the book.

Performing poetry

This is a hugely enjoyable rhyme to read together as a piece of whole class choral reading. First re-present it as an enlarged text such as a poster so that the words can be seen as a whole. Try out different ways of grouping the class to read aloud the different sections of the poem. You might, for example, ask pairs or groups of children to read pairs of lines while everyone reads the repeated refrains 'But Mister Magnolia has only one boot!' Add instrumental accompaniment and present a musical version to another class or for assembly.

In guided reading groups of children can go on to prepare their own version for performance.

Booktalk and role-play

Talk with the children about their responses to the whole story focussing first on their likes and dislikes.

Is there anything about the way that the story is written or the language that Quentin Blake uses that they particularly liked?

Were they puzzled by anything in the story?

Collect the children's responses into the class reading journal.

Go into role as the exhuberant and flamboyant Mister Magnolia responding to the spirit of the children's initial comments and questions and encourage them to ask further questions for you to answer.

Session six:

Drawing and painting

Tell children about the way in which
Quentin Blake works. He has described this as a
process in which he draws his pictures and then
paints onto them using watercolour.
Explain that they are going to have a go at
painting in the style of Quentin Blake.
Give them fine black pens and ask them to draw a
picture of one of the characters from the story or
one of the events it depicts. Enlarge the drawings.
Children can go on to paint in watercolour.

Session seven:

Shared writing

Using a flip chart and, with you acting as scribe to
help shape the children's ideas, write another
verse or two to insert into the poem. Use the
original framework.

" Mister Magnolia has only one boot
   He has a…..
   And…..

But Mister Magnolia has only one boot."

Children should go on to illustrate the new
ideas and pin up the finished verses as part of
the display.

Sessions eight and nine:

Storytelling, bookmaking

What did happen to Mister Magnolia's new boot?

Put children into pairs to make up the story of the
missing boot. Some of these stories can be shared
with the whole class before being written in
individual home-made books. Once they have
finished, ask children to read their story to two
friends before adding it to the class display for
everyone to read.

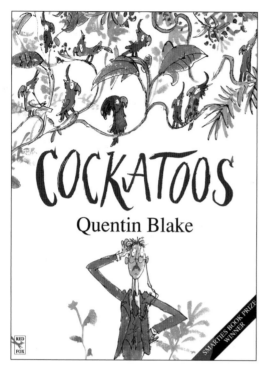

COCKATOOS

This book is a sophisticated counting book from 0-10 as well as an enjoyable game of hide and seek. In this the readers are enlisted to be part of the game, but with more success than poor Professor Dupont whose bewilderment is so well depicted.

Session ten:

Storytelling

Quentin Blake says, 'The interesting thing about drawing my own books is that it's really a story in pictures, with the necessary words underneath.' Talk with the children about whether they agree with this and then test this comment out with the book *Cockatoos*. Using scanned pictures make a wordless version of the book and, after reading the first page aloud to set the scene, 'read' through it as a class making up the story together from the pictures as you go.

Session eleven:

Performance

Introduce Professor Dupont to the class and extravagantly model for them the way that he likes to greet his cockatoos in the morning. Now read *Cockatoos* aloud to the class inviting everyone to join in the hunt for the missing cockatoos and with the repeated phrasing and patterning of the story.

Encourage the children to mimic the actions of Professor Dupont as he searches through the house.

Session twelve:

Booktalk

Discuss the book with the class focussing first on their likes and dislikes and then on the things that puzzle them.

What do they think the last sentence means?

Session thirteen:

Responding to illustration

Give pairs of children a laminated photocopy of pictures of one of the rooms of the house and ask them to examine it closely to see what it contains. Give them a list of things to look for, for example:

Can they find something that makes them laugh? Something that they think is in the wrong room? Something that they really like? Something that they don't like? Something old and something new? Something that they would like to have in their own home?

Finally, ask each of them to draw their favourite thing from the picture in the style of Quentin Blake.

Invite children to talk about what they found in their picture with the rest of the class.

Mind-mapping

How do you know this book is by Quentin Blake? What makes his work so recognisable?

Using shared writing, put the name 'Quentin Blake' in the middle of a large sheet of paper and with the children's help try to map out those aspects that the children think define his work; they might suggest aspects such as colour, what his characters are like, what his books are about, the settings he chooses, or the imagery and language that he uses in his books. As children suggest things, try and group them together although as this is a discussion about the things that the children have noticed they probably won't fit easily into neat categories. Pin the poster up to be added to later in the project.

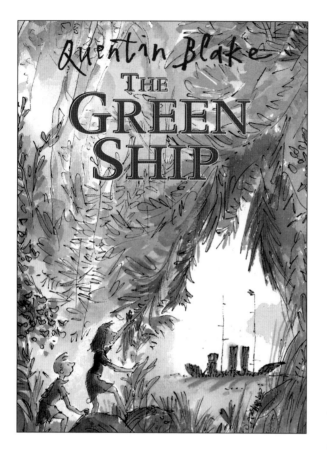

THE GREEN SHIP

When staying with their aunt one summer two children find their way into a hidden garden. In it they find a wonderful ship made from growing trees and shrubs. Their play on board it leads to a series of glorious imaginary voyages as well as some new relationships and a lifelong memory. This is a book about growing up and moving from childhood into the adult world.
Children will enjoy this book's inventiveness and its creation of a rich other world of the imagination.

This book will need to be read aloud to the children several times over the period of the work so that they get to know it very well.

Session one:

Story mapping

After reading the story aloud, ask children to work in pairs to retell the story between them. Using a flip chart, draw a shared story map to show the key events of the story. Talk with the children about what the characters and setting are like and then re-read the story.

Sessions two and three:

Storytelling, story mapping

Make a storytelling circle and retell the story with you as narrator. Stop at important parts of the story and ask children to go into the middle of the circle to act it out. Children can then go on to draw their own story maps. They should annotate these, perhaps adding detail about events, characters or places and adding speech and thought bubbles.

Session four:

Responding to illustration

Using prepared scanned and laminated pictures, ask groups of children to look at individual pictures closely and talk together about what they can see and how it makes them feel. The storm scene or the last picture of the overgrown ship are strong images to use.

Ask each group to tell you what they noticed and thought about, listing comments onto a flipchart or into the class reading journal. Talk together about how different and similar different groups' ideas are.

Session five:

Drama and role-play, writing in role

Go into role as Alice and have a conversation with the class as if they were her brother walking home after playing at the end of the first day.

In role, ask the children to write the letter that Alice might have written to her mother telling her about their discovery of the ship.

Re-enactment through play

Story boxes
Make a ship story box and introduce it to the class. Groups could play with this to retell the story or to tell their own stories. These could be written down or taped and shared with the class.

Role-play

With the children's help turn the role-play area
into a ship. This will create lots of opportunities
for writing, both as part of the play and as a more
teacher-directed activity. You could, for example,
join the children aboard the ship to write a postcard in role or ask children to write postcards
from their last journey as a writing activity.
Other writing opportunities include: a ship's log,
including an entry detailing surviving the storm,
a poster advertising for a ship's crew, a list of the
jobs the ship's crew have to do each day,
instructions for swabbing the deck or an
annotated map, showing the route of a journey.

Session six:

Drawing and annotating

Suggest pairs of children choose one of the
characters to draw, annotating them to show what
they are like. Share what the children have done,
and ask individuals to talk about their pictures.

Session seven:

Shared writing

Begin to write a shared poem about either the
storm or the overgrown ship.
Revisit the notes of the previous conversations
when the children were talking around the
pictures in session four; you might use a line
from the book as a starting point, for example
'what a storm it was!', or 'year by year the trees
are growing back into their old shape...'

Session eight:

Painting

Suggest children paint their own green ships mix-
ing different shades of green and experimenting
with a variety of media and material.

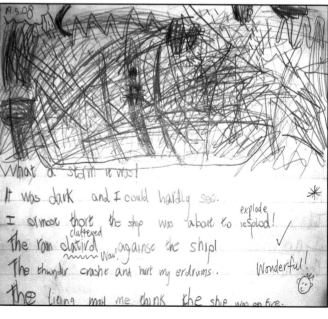

Sessions nine, ten and eleven:

Writing in role

Ask children to go into role as Alice or her brother
to act out the beginning of the story while you
read it out loud as narrator. Stop at the point
where the ship comes into view. Go round the
room and ask children to say what they can see.
In role as either Alice or her brother, children can
now write the story into pre-prepared books. Less
experienced writers could make a group book in
shared writing while more experienced ones work
in guided writing to write and illustrate individual
books. Share the books when they are finished
and place them in the book corner.

Sessions twelve and thirteen:

Booktalk

Quentin Blake was chosen to be the first
Children's Laureate and is widely regarded to be
'the best-loved children's illustrator'.
Discuss with the children whether they would
agree with this.

Ask the class to look back over the work that they
have done as part of this author study and to talk
to a partner about something that they have particularly enjoyed.

What do they think they have learned?

Ask them to write one sentence each about both
of these questions.
Invite children to share their views with each
other before displaying them alongside the class's
work in a final celebration.

Acknowledgements

We thank the following:
For permission to use examples of their children's work in this book:

Mei Ching Bastian
Stamford Hill Primary School, Haringey
Matt Park
Ashmead Primary School, Lewisham
Luke Page
Westbridge Primary School, Wandsworth
Lucy Love
Hill Mead Primary School, Lambeth
Abigail Freedman
North West London Jewish Day School, Barnet
David Gilbert
Britannia Village Primary School, Newham
Daiva Quinn
Kensal Rise Primary School, Brent
Jennie Hopkins
Archbishop Sumner Primary School, Lambeth
Margaret Doherty
St Mary's R.C.Primary School, Brent
Jane Kleyn
Chadwell St.Mary's C of E Primary School, Essex
Heather Turner
Star Primary School, Newham
Debbie Fadipe
Our Lady of Grace Infants School, Brent
Ann Driscoll
Oliver Goldsmiths Primary School, Brent
Jennifer Atkinson
Applegarth Infants School, Croydon
Wendy Green
Drew Primary School, Brent
Catherine Gdula
Edmund Waller Primary School, Lewisham
Ashmount Infants School, Islington
Broadmead Infants School, Croydon
Wigton Primary School, Cumbria

For permission to use examples of classrooms at work:
Archbishop Sumner Primary School, Lambeth
Ashmead Primary School, Lewisham
Stamford Hill Primary School, Haringey

For her work: **Zoë Luchmun**

For kind permission to use illustrations

Beegu
illustration © Alexis Deacon
Random House Children's Books, 2003

Traction Man is Here
illustration © Mini Grey
Random House Children's Books, 2005

The Owl and the Pussy Cat
illustration © Louise Voce
Walker Books, 1991

No Dinner!
illustration © Jessica Souhami
Frances Lincoln Ltd,1999

The Story Tree
Illustration © Sophie Fatus
Barefoot Books Ltd, 2001

Jamela's Dress
illustration © Niki Daly
Frances Lincoln Ltd, 1999

Aaaarrgghh, Spider!
illustration © Lydia Monks
Egmont UK Ltd, 2004

Where the Wild Things Are
illustration © Maurice Sendak
Random House Children's Books, 1967

The Snail and the Whale
illustration © Axel Scheffler
Macmillan Children's Books, 2003

Cockatoos
illustration © Quentin Blake
Random House Children's Books, 1992

Mister Magnolia
illustration © Quentin Blake
Random House Children's Books, 1980

The Green Ship
illustration © Quentin Blake
Random House Children's Books, 1998